Contents

Chapter 1 – HTML and the Internet   2

Chapter 2 – Writing HTML   9

Chapter 3 – Graphics and Fonts   17

Chapter 4 – Colours and Hyperlinks   25

Chapter 5 – Page Layout with Tables   36

Chapter 6 – Building your Home Page   43

Chapter 7 – Multimedia   53

Chapter 8 – Uploading by FTP   58

Index   64

Chapter 1
HTML and the Internet

What is HTML?

HTML is the language of the web – every page you visit on the Internet is powered by HTML.

The name stands for **HyperText Markup Language**, a special computer language designed for the Internet. It is simple to use and has many advanced features that make the Internet what it is today.

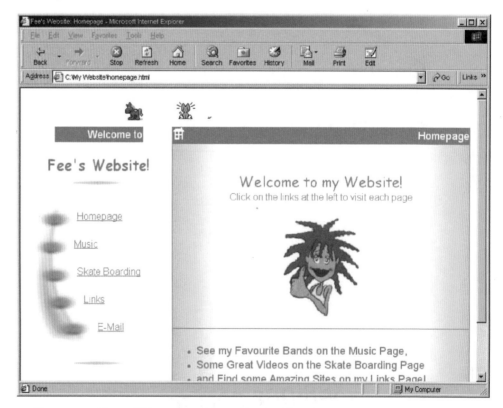

Figure 1.1: You will have made a web site like this by the end of the book!

Web pages

The information on the Internet is in the form of billions of web sites. Each web site is made up from different parts, like pages of a book, and they are called web pages.

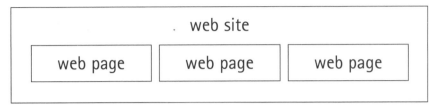

Figure 1.2

When you make a web site, you save it onto a server somewhere so that anyone who wants to can go and see it.

The best web sites, such as **http://www.nasa.gov** and **http://www.something.com**, have thousands of hits every day. When you make your own web site, try to think of something original that will make other people want to visit it. You can also advertise your web site so that people using search engines like **http://www.google.com** can find it if you share an interest in something.

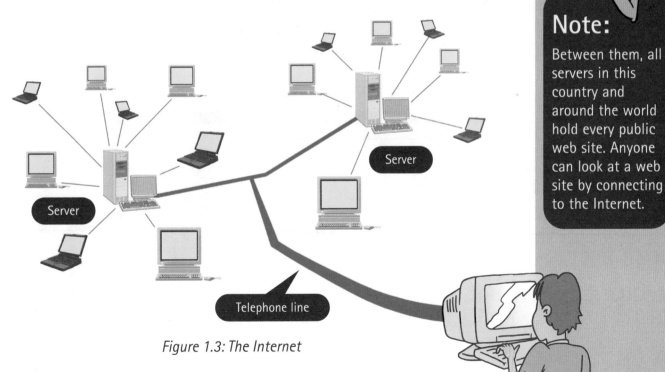

Figure 1.3: The Internet

Although every web page of every web site looks different, underneath, they all use HTML!

Note:

The Internet is sometimes called the World Wide Web or WWW for short. It lets many computers talk to each other and share information.

Note:

Between them, all servers in this country and around the world hold every public web site. Anyone can look at a web site by connecting to the Internet.

Is HTML difficult to learn?

No! It's easy. That's why there are so many web sites out there. All you need is a text editor, like Notepad, and a browser, like Internet Explorer.

HTML is a special code or computer "language" that you will learn to use by reading this book.

The great thing about HTML is that people who visit your web site don't have to see all the bits of code that you have written – they just see nice-looking web pages. That is because:

 When you open an HTML file in an editor, you can see the code.

 But if you open the same HTML file in a browser, you see the final page.

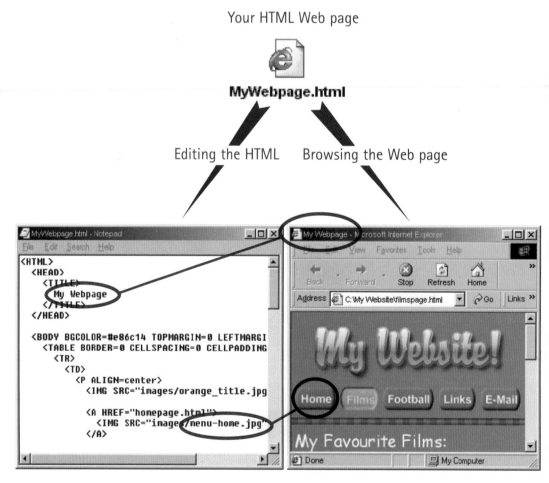

Figure 1.4: The HTML code that makes up a web page

As you work through the examples in the next few chapters, you will soon understand the jumble of letters and numbers in Figure 1.4.

Other methods

There are lots of programs around that can write all the code for you, hiding it so you never even know it's there! These include FrontPage, FireWorks, Word, WordPerfect, Publisher and many more.

They let you edit a web page easily, just like any other document. There are, however, lots of advantages in writing the code yourself in HTML:

 You know exactly what you put in, so nothing else is adding extra clutter which slows down your pages.

Result: Your web site loads more quickly.

 You pay more attention to the layout because you have to think about it first.

Result: Your web pages look better and are easier to navigate.

 You are not limited in what you can do - the whole web site is up to you!

Result: You can add better, newer features to your web pages.

 You will learn about software design and how to control what a computer can do.

Result: You understand more about how the Web works.

Eye-catching designs

Many of the commands in HTML perform simple word processing tasks such as:

 make text bold, italic or underlined

 align text left, right or centre

 create lists, bullet-points and headings

 change the colour or size of text

 insert pictures and graphics

Normal Text		
Bold Text		
Italic Text		
<u>Underlined</u> Text		
Left		
	Centre	
		Right
1	2	3

Using HTML you can also insert:

 animations, films and videos

 sound clips and background music

 colours, textures or images as backgrounds

 interactive links and buttons that allow people to move around and visit all the different parts of your web site

 online games using **Java** and **Flash** technologies

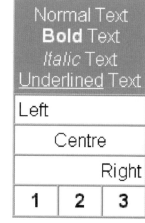

Your own web site

By the end of this book, you will have made your own web site about whatever you like and in any style you choose. Chapter by chapter you will add new features that continually extend your knowledge of HTML.

 Log on to **www.payne-gallway.co.uk/basichtml/web site** and explore it. You are going to make a web site just like it, except yours will be even better!

 Log off when you have explored the web site.

Software you will need

 A text editor such as **Notepad** to write the code.

Figure 1.5: Notepad

 A web browser.

Internet Explorer can be used for this, although **Netscape Navigator** or **Opera** will work fine, too.

Figure 1.6: Internet Explorer

Tip:
A **browser** is a tool that lets you view a web page on the Internet or on your computer.

Creating new folders

You will need some new folders to hold your web site elements.

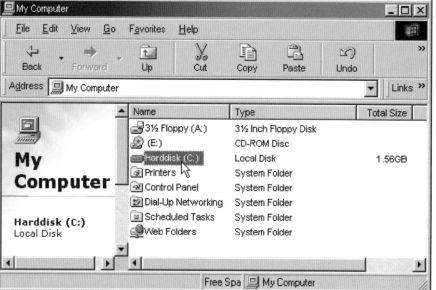

Double-click the **My Computer** icon on your desktop.

Double-click the **Hard disk (C:)** icon.

Figure 1.7: Double-click on the C: icon

From the File menu, select **New, Folder**. Type **My Website** and press **Enter** to name the new folder.

Double-click the new **My Website** folder to open it.

Make three new folders in here called **Images**, **Videos** and **Sounds**.

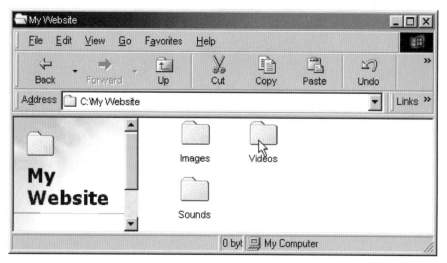

Figure 1.8: Your three important folders

Tip:
If you make a mistake, you can always change the name of a folder by right-clicking on its icon and selecting **Rename**.

Now you are ready to start building your web site!

Chapter 2
Writing HTML

HTML tags

In this chapter you will create your first web page. It will eventually look like this:

Figure 2.1: Splash Page

The web page in Figure 2.1 is called a splash page. It welcomes visitors to your site and should give some information about what it is about.

Web pages contain elements such as paragraphs, tables, images and so on. These elements are created using HTML **tags**.

Start tags and end tags

In HTML there are two types of tag: **start tags** and **end tags**, and most elements have both a start tag and an end tag. Both types of tag are written inside angled brackets <>. End tags start with a forward slash (/) inside the angled brackets.

 Open Notepad by clicking **Start, Programs, Accessories, Notepad**.

 Follow the instructions below to type the text shown in Figure 2.2:

```
splash.html - Notepad

File   Edit   Search   Help

<HTML>
  <HEAD>
    <TITLE>Fee's Website: Welcome</TITLE>
  </HEAD>

  <BODY>
    <P>
      Welcome to My Website!
    </P>
  </BODY>
</HTML>
```

Figure 2.2: Your first code

 Type the first line <HTML>. This is an example of an HTML **tag**. <HTML> tells your browser that you are writing an HTML document.

Press **Enter**, then two spaces.
Type <HEAD>. This will start the header of your page.

Press **Enter**, and then four spaces.
Type <TITLE> followed by **Fee's Website: Welcome**

Type a </TITLE> tag. This will close the TITLE section. Then add </HEAD> to close the header section.

As you can see, writing HTML is really just putting different bits of information in little sections.

First of all you started an HTML section by using the <HTML> tag. Inside that HTML section you added a header section, and in the header section you set the title. Once each section is done, you close it with a tag starting with a / (forward slash) character, like </TITLE>

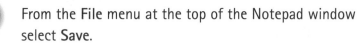 Now type the rest of the text so that your Notepad window looks exactly the same as Figure 2.2.
First you are adding a body section with the <BODY> tag. Inside the body is a paragraph, which you write with the <P> tag.

 Don't forget to end the page with </HTML>.

Saving your work

 From the File menu at the top of the Notepad window select Save.

 Find the My Website folder you made in Chapter 1.

Set the file type to All Files. Name the file splash.html. Click Save.

Figure 2.3: Saving your file

Viewing in a browser

Now you have typed some HTML and saved it, you can see what it will look like in a browser.

 Minimise Notepad.

 Double-click the **My Computer** icon on your desktop.

 Find the **My Website** folder and open it.

Double-click **splash.html** to open it:

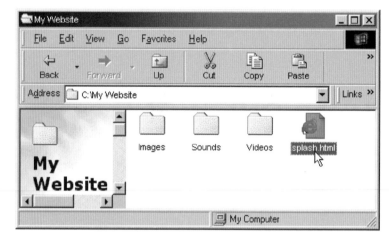

Figure 2.4

A browser window appears on your screen, like this:

This is what you type between the
`<TITLE>` and `</TITLE>` tags

This is the paragraph you typed inside the `<BODY>` section

Figure 2.5: Browsing your first web page

OK - so it doesn't look much at the moment, but pretty soon you will be adding pictures and much more.

Tip:
The font may be different on your computer - don't worry about this. You'll learn how to change it in Chapter 3.

The **browser** has read your HTML tags, followed their instructions, and displayed a web page. This is called **interpreting** your code.

For anything you do in HTML, follow the three main steps:

 Write some HTML in Notepad.

Save it.

View the page in a browser.

Using parameters

 Minimise the browser window and **restore** Notepad by clicking its icon on the **taskbar**.

Start | splash.html - Notepad | **Fee's Website: Welco...**

Figure 2.6: Restoring Notepad

Look at the paragraph of text in the body section:

```
<BODY>
  <P>
    Welcome to My Website!
  </P>
</BODY>
```

To change the way an object looks using HTML, you must extend a tag with a parameter and a value. In this example, the <P> tag will be extended with an ALIGN parameter. The value of the alignment is CENTER.

Spell CENTER the American way!

```
<BODY>
  <P ALIGN=CENTER>
    Welcome to My Website!
  </P>
</BODY>
```

> **Tip:**
> The ALIGN parameter of the <P> tag can be one of three values: LEFT, CENTER, or RIGHT.

 Change **your** <P> tag to <P ALIGN=CENTER>

Save the file and minimise Notepad.

Restore the browser window by clicking on the browser icon on the taskbar.

Refreshing the page

Refresh

Tip:

Holding **Shift** whilst you refresh the page forces the browser to load the page all over again. Otherwise it might not bother!

▶ Hold down **Shift** and click the **Refresh** or **Reload** button in the browser.

Fee's Website: Welcome - Microsoft Internet Explorer - [Working Offline]   _ □ ×

File   Edit   View   Favorites   Tools   Help

Back   Forward   Stop   Refresh   Home   Search   Favorites   History

Address   C:\My Website\splash.html   Go   Links »

Welcome to My Website!

Done   My Computer

Figure 2.7: Centred Text

Adding more paragraphs

Now add another centred paragraph below this one.

▶ Go back to Notepad and find the paragraph you just centred.

```
<BODY>
  <P ALIGN=CENTER>
    Welcome to My Website!
  </P>
</BODY>
```

▶ Add another paragraph after it so the **<BODY>** section reads exactly like Figure 2.8:

```
<BODY>
  <P ALIGN=CENTER>
    Welcome to My Website
  </P>
  <P ALIGN=CENTER>
    This is Fee's Website
    and is all about:
    My Favourite Bands,
    Skate Boarding
    and Internet Games
  </P>
</BODY>
```

Figure 2.8: A second paragraph

14

Save the file and **Shift + Refresh** the **splash.html** web page in your browser.

Figure 2.9: How the two paragraphs are displayed

You will see that the browser has ignored where you pressed **Enter** to separate each line of text in Figure 2.8!

The <BR> tag

 To solve this problem, type a <BR> tag in Notepad where you want a new line.

```
<P ALIGN=CENTER>
  This is Fee's Website<BR>
  and is all about:<BR>
  My Favourite Bands,<BR>
  Skate Boarding<BR>
  and Internet Games
</P>
```

 Save these changes and refresh your page again.

Figure 2.10: Using <BR> tags to separate lines of text

 Now your page is shown properly with new lines where they should be.

Graphics for your web pages

In Chapter 3 you will learn how to add some cool graphics, but first you need to know where to get them!

 Load Internet Explorer and go to:
www.payne-gallway.co.uk/basichtml/graphics

 Click on the link called **Images for splash.html** and wait for the new page to load.

Right-click on the image called **my-picture-1.jpg** and select **Save Picture As** or **Save Image As** from the drop-down menu:

```
Open Link
Open Link in New Window
Save Target As...
Print Target

Show Picture
Save Picture As...
Set as Wallpaper
Set as Desktop Item...

Cut
Copy
Copy Shortcut
Paste

Add to Favorites...

Properties
```

Figure 2.11: my-picture-1.jpg

 Click on **C:** in the list called **Save in:**

Save in: 🖴 Harddisk (C:) ▾

Different icons should appear in the main part of the window.

Double-click the **My Website** icon, then double-click **Images**.

Save in: should look like this:

Save in: 📁 Images ▾

Press **Save** to download **my-picture-1.jpg** to your **Images** folder.

 Close your browser and **disconnect** from the Internet.

Chapter 3
Graphics and Fonts

Important!

When you open an HTML file using Notepad, don't forget to select **All Files (*.*)** from the list called **Files of type**.

In this Chapter you will add some simple graphics to splash.html and learn how to use different fonts.

 Open Notepad (**Start, Programs, Accessories, Notepad**) if it is not already running.

 Select **Open** from the **File** menu and find your **splash.html** file.

 Find the two paragraphs that you typed in Chapter 2. Add this paragraph between them:

```
<P ALIGN=CENTER>
   Welcome to My Website!
</P>
<P ALIGN=CENTER>
   <IMG SRC="images/my-picture-1.jpg">
</P>
<P ALIGN=CENTER>
   This is Fee's Website<BR>
   and is all about:<BR>
   My Favourite Bands,<BR>
   Skate Boarding<BR>
   and Internet Games
</P>
```

Figure 3.1

Tip:

To view the file in your browser:

- Double-click **My Computer** from the **Desktop**

- Go into the **My Website** folder

- Double-click the **splash.html** icon

 Save **splash.html** and view it in your browser.

Tip:

If your page doesn't look like Figure 3.2, try downloading **my picture-1.jpg** again and make sure you are saving it into the **Images** folder you made in Chapter 1.

Also check that you typed the text shown in Figure 3.1 properly.

Your web page should now include the picture you downloaded at the end of Chapter 2:

Figure 3.2: Your first graphic

<IMG> tags

In Notepad, look at the tag you added to the new paragraph. It is the <IMG> tag which, you guessed it, stands for **image**. The SRC parameter tells the browser which image to show.

<IMG SRC="images/my-picture-1.jpg">

Your **images** folder

The picture of Fee you downloaded

Two other useful parameters of the <IMG> tag are WIDTH and HEIGHT. They can be used to stretch the picture.

 Add these two parameters to your <IMG> tag:

<IMG SRC="images/my-picture-1.jpg" **WIDTH=400 HEIGHT=80>**

400 pixels wide

80 pixels high

Tip:

In HTML, the width and height of a picture are measured in **pixels**, short for **picture elements**. A pixel is one of the tiny coloured dots that make up your screen.

 Save and then refresh your web page. Fee should look like this:

Figure 3.3: Play around with the WIDTH and HEIGHT values

18

Correct image sizes

Even if you don't want to stretch the picture, it is best to add WIDTH and HEIGHT parameters so the browser knows how much space to leave for the picture.

But how do you know what size the picture is supposed to be?

Open Paint (**Start**, **Programs**, **Accessories**, **Paint**). ——————

From the **File** menu select **Open** and find your **Images** folder.

Set the file filter to **All Picture Files**:

Files of type: All Picture Files   ▼

Select **my-picture-1.jpg** and click **Open**. ————————   Open
Fee's picture should appear in the Paint program.

From the **Image** menu choose **Attributes...**

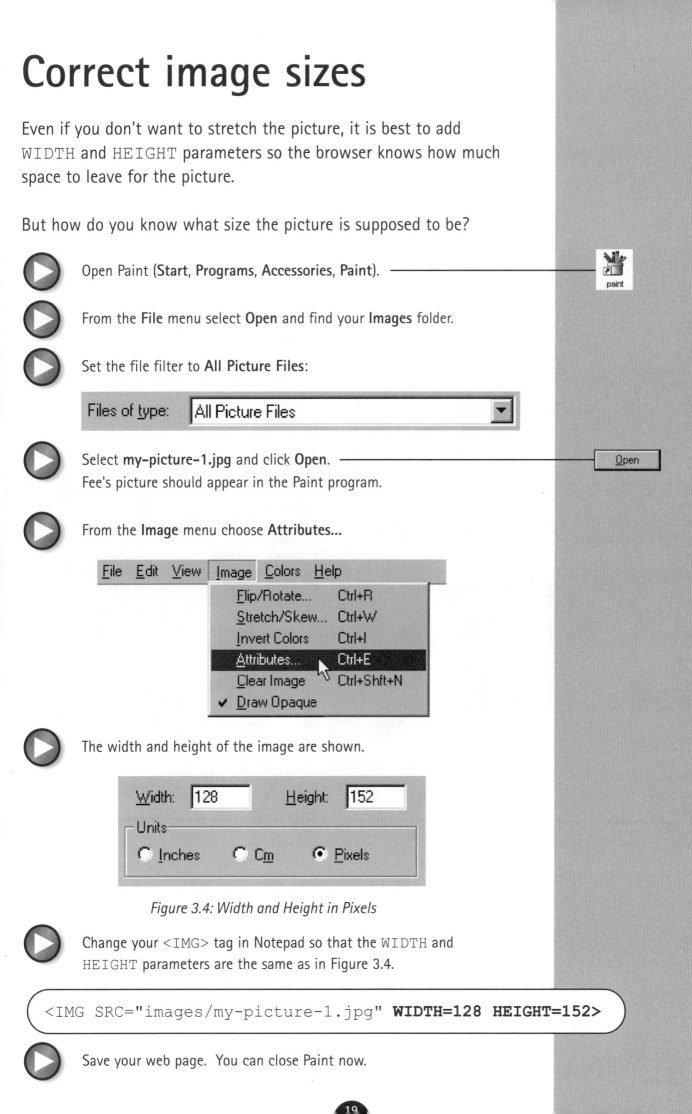

The width and height of the image are shown.

Width: 128   Height: 152
Units
○ Inches   ○ Cm   ⦿ Pixels

Figure 3.4: Width and Height in Pixels

Change your <IMG> tag in Notepad so that the WIDTH and HEIGHT parameters are the same as in Figure 3.4.

```
<IMG SRC="images/my-picture-1.jpg" WIDTH=128 HEIGHT=152>
```

Save your web page. You can close Paint now.

Textured backgrounds

 Connect to the Internet.

 Go to **www.payne-gallway.co.uk/basichtml/graphics** on the Internet and click the **Images for splash.html** link.

 Download **texture.jpg** and **blue-bg.jpg** into your **Images** folder.

 Return to Notepad and in your **splash.html** file find the <BODY> tag. Add a BACKGROUND parameter like this:

```
<BODY BACKGROUND="images/texture.jpg">
```

Save **splash.html** and **Shift + Refresh** the page in your browser.

> This texture makes the page very difficult to read, and clashes with the white area of the picture!

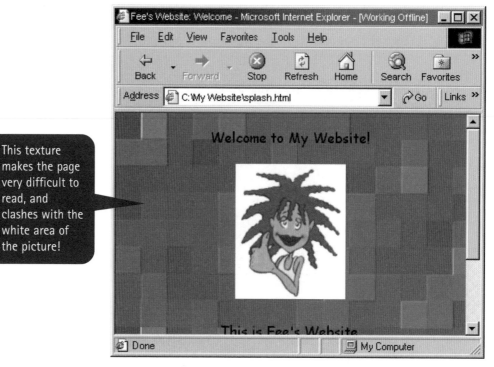

Figure 3.5: A Background texture for splash.html

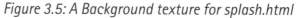 Now delete the BACKGROUND parameter in Notepad so that the tag looks exactly like this: <BODY>

 Save your work. You will use a better background texture later on.

Basic font properties

Bold, italic and underlined text can come in very useful, and they are very easy to apply in HTML.

 Look at the first paragraph in your web page and add these tags:

```
<P ALIGN=CENTER>
   <B>Welcome</B> to <I>My</I> <U>Website!</U>
</P>
```

 Save the page and refresh it in your browser:

Welcome to *My* <u>Website!</u>

Can you see how `<B>` makes bold, `<I>` makes italic and `<U>` makes underline?

 Now edit the paragraph so it reads like this:

```
<P ALIGN=CENTER>
   <U>Welcome</U> to <B><I>My</I><U>Website!</U></B>
</P>
```

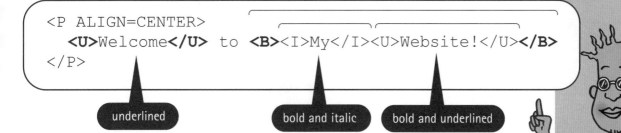

underlined   bold and italic   bold and underlined

 After saving it, refresh your browser:

<u>Welcome</u> to ***My*** <u>**Website!**</u>

 Now go back to Notepad and remove all `<B>`, `<I>` and `<U>` tags so it is just a plain paragraph again.

Tip:
Don't forget to close each section with `</B>`, `</I>` or `</U>`.

As you can see - it is possible to have any section inside any other section to combine different effects.

The <FONT> tag

To change any other property of the text in your web page, use the <FONT> tag.

 Make your first paragraph look like the example below, then save your code.

```
<P ALIGN=CENTER>
  <FONT SIZE=5 FACE="arial">Welcome to My Website!</FONT>
</P>
```

 Refresh your browser - your page should look like this now:

Figure 3.6: Using the <FONT> tag

Font size

The size of a font in HTML can be set from one up to seven and the default size is three:

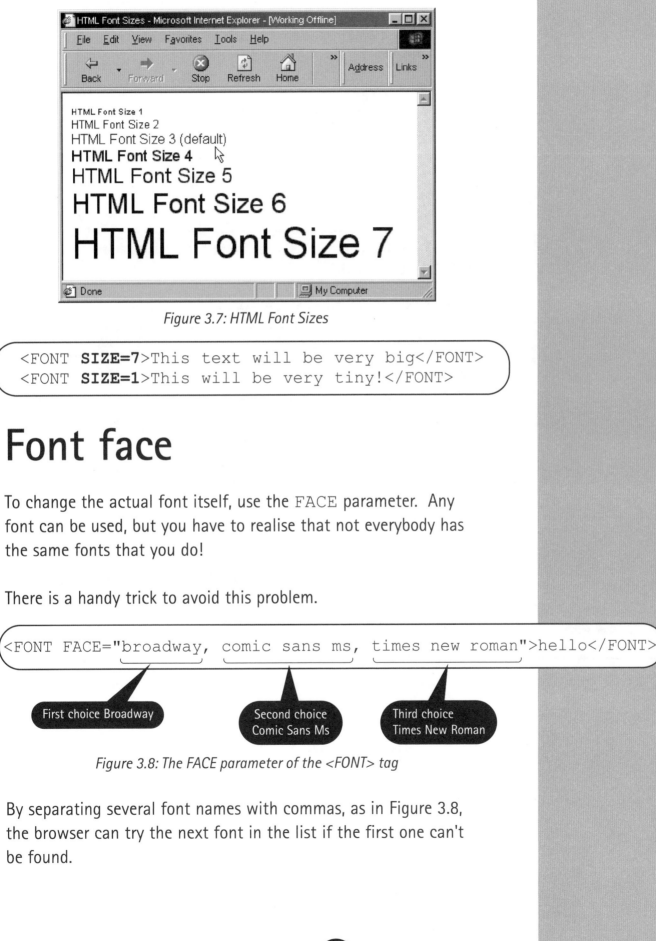

Figure 3.7: HTML Font Sizes

```
<FONT SIZE=7>This text will be very big</FONT>
<FONT SIZE=1>This will be very tiny!</FONT>
```

Font face

To change the actual font itself, use the FACE parameter. Any font can be used, but you have to realise that not everybody has the same fonts that you do!

There is a handy trick to avoid this problem.

```
<FONT FACE="broadway, comic sans ms, times new roman">hello</FONT>
```

First choice Broadway

Second choice
Comic Sans Ms

Third choice
Times New Roman

Figure 3.8: The FACE parameter of the <FONT> tag

By separating several font names with commas, as in Figure 3.8, the browser can try the next font in the list if the first one can't be found.

Fonts for splash.html

 In Notepad, find the last paragraph of text.
Modify the font properties like this:

```
<P>
   <FONT SIZE=3 FACE="arial">
      This is Fee's Website<BR>
      and is all about<BR>
   </FONT>
   <FONT SIZE=4 FACE="arial">
      My Favourite Bands,<BR>
      Skate Boarding<BR>
      and Internet Games!
   </FONT>
</P>
```

Then change the <FONT> tag in the first paragraph on the page from this:

```
<FONT SIZE=5 FACE="arial">Welcome to...
```

to this:

```
<FONT SIZE=5 FACE="comic sans ms, arial">Welcome to...
```

Save the file and see how it looks in your browser.

Check your code!

You have done quite a lot already so, to make sure that you haven't missed anything out, check your code against Figure 3.9 below.

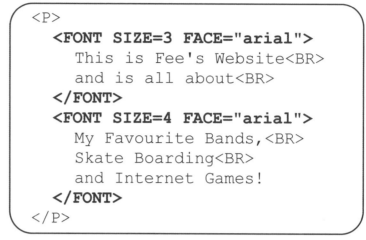

```
splash.html - Notepad                                          _ □ ×
File   Edit   Search   Help
<HTML>
  <HEAD>
    <TITLE>Fee's Website: Welcome</TITLE>
  </HEAD>

  <BODY>
    <P ALIGN=CENTER>
      <FONT SIZE=5 FACE="comic sans ms, arial">Welcome to My Website!</FONT>
    <P ALIGN=CENTER>
      <IMG SRC="images/my-picture-1.jpg" WIDTH=128 HEIGHT=152>
    </P>
    <P ALIGN=CENTER>
      <FONT SIZE=3 FACE="arial">
      This is Fee's Website<BR>
      and is all about:<BR>
      </FONT>
      <FONT SIZE=4 FACE="arial">
      My Favourite Bands,<BR>
      Skate Boarding<BR>
      and Internet Games
      </FONT>
    </P>
  </BODY>
</HTML>
```

Figure 3.9: The full HTML code so far

Chapter 4

Colours and Hyperlinks

It is very simple to add colours to a web page.

There are 16 preset colours that you can use straight away, and custom colours that you can mix yourself!

Aqua	Black	Blue	Fuschia	Gray	Green	Lime	Maroon

Navy	Olive	Purple	Red	Silver	Teal	White	Yellow

Figure 4.1: Preset HTML Colours

 Make sure Notepad is open and showing your **splash.html** file.

Double-click **My Computer** from the desktop and find the **My Website** folder if it's not on your screen already. Double-click **splash.html** to launch the web page in your browser.

Changing background colour

To paint a background, add a BGCOLOR parameter to the <BODY> tag. BGCOLOR stands for **background colour**, and its value can be any of the 16 preset colours from Figure 4.1.

It works in a similar way to the BACKGROUND parameter you tried in Chapter 3.

 In Notepad, add a BGCOLOR parameter with value TEAL to your <BODY> tag. It should look like this:

```
<BODY BGCOLOR=TEAL>
```

Tip:
You must always type **COLOR** instead of **COLOUR** when you use HTML!

Save your page and see how it looks by pressing the **Refresh** button whilst holding **Shift** in your browser.

Figure 4.2: A TEAL background

 Try out some different coloured backgrounds and see how they look!

 Now set the background back to white, using the WHITE value of the BGCOLOR parameter:

<BODY BGCOLOR=**WHITE**>

Changing text colour

Setting the main text colour is just like painting the background, except you use the TEXT parameter instead of BGCOLOR.

 Edit the <BODY> tag like this:

<BODY BGCOLOR=WHITE **TEXT=MAROON**>

 Save the HTML and press **Shift** and **Refresh** in your browser. The text shouldn't be black any more!

Colours with <FONT> tags

The <FONT> tag has another useful feature which allows you to change the colour of individual bits of text in your document.

 There should be two <FONT> sections in the last paragraph of your HTML file. The bottom one looks like this:

> <FONT SIZE=4 FACE="arial">

 Add a COLOR parameter to it:

> <FONT SIZE=4 FACE="arial" **COLOR=RED**>

> After saving, see how the text inside that section has changed colour. (Don't forget to press **Shift + Refresh** again!)

Figure 4.3: Using the COLOR parameter of the <FONT> tag

27

Hexadecimal numbers

Although it is very quick to just type in the name of the colour you want, 16 colours isn't really enough to design really stylish web pages.

This is where the hexadecimal system is useful: it will let you choose from over 16 *million* colours!

Hexadecimal numbers (**hex** for short) don't go from 0 to 9 like normal numbers do. They start at **0** and end at **F** – yes, they use letters too! – like this:

Normal Numbers	0	1	2	3	4	5	6	7	8	9	10	11	12	13	14	15
Hexadecimal	0	1	2	3	4	5	6	7	8	9	A	B	C	D	E	F

Figure 4.4: Hexadecimal Number System

In HTML, hex numbers are put together in pairs that go from **00** up to **FF** in 256 steps:

Tip:
The little arrows in Figure 4.5 mean that the pattern continues the same way.

0.	00	16.	10	32.	20	240.	F0
1.	01	17.	11	33.	21	241.	F1
2.	02	18.	12	34.	22	242.	F2
3.	03	19.	13	35.	23	243.	F3
4.	04	20.	14	36.	24	244.	F4
5.	05	21.	15	37.	25	245.	F5
6.	06	22.	16	↓		246.	F6
7.	07	23.	17	215.	D7	247.	F7
8.	08	24.	18	216.	D8	248.	F8
9.	09	25.	19	217.	D9	249.	F9
10.	0A	26.	1A	218.	DA	250.	FA
11.	0B	27.	1B	219.	DB	251.	FB
12.	0C	28.	1C	↓		252.	FC
13.	0D	29.	1D	237.	ED	253.	FD
14.	0E	30.	1E	238.	EE	254.	FE
15.	0F	31.	1F	239.	EF	255.	FF

Figure 4.5: The 256 steps from 00 to FF

HTML colours using hex

Imagine that you are painting on a **black** canvas. Every time you put some colour on the canvas, it gets brighter (because no matter what colour you add, it's always brighter than black).

We can use hex pairs to describe a colour by saying that **00** isn't putting any paint on the canvas, so it stays dark, whereas **FF** is splashing loads of paint on the canvas, so it gets very bright. All the other hex numbers in between will give different shades of a colour from dark to bright.

A hex colour is written like this:

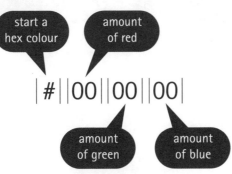

Figure 4.6: Mixing hex colours

This is tricky to understand, but you'll get the hang of it in no time!

The # symbol (near the **Enter** key on your keyboard) tells the browser we want a hexadecimal colour. Then there is a hex pair for the amount of red, another hex pair for green and another for blue.

Try it out

 Find the <BODY> tag in your HTML file, **splash.html**. It looks like this:

```
<BODY BGCOLOR=WHITE TEXT=MAROON>
```

 Now change it to use these hexadecimal colours:

```
<BODY BGCOLOR=#000000 TEXT=#FFFFFF>
```

Save the code and see how the browser interprets the new
`<BODY>` tag:

Figure 4.7: Your first hex colours

The background is just like a black canvas because no colour
was added:

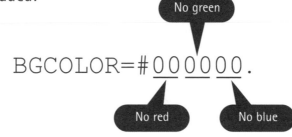

The text is bright white because the amount of red, green and blue
are full: TEXT=#FFFFFF.

Here are some of the pre-set colours in hex form so you can see
how the hexadecimal system works:

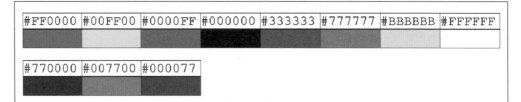

Figure 4.8: Basic hexadecimal colours

Remember that FF
is maximum
colour, **77** is
about half-way up
the scale and **00**
is no colour.

If you're still not quite sure what all these fiddly little numbers and letters mean, try some of them out in the <BODY> or <FONT> tags to get used to them. Then experiment with your own hex combinations.

If you are really stuck, click on the **Help With Hex** link at **www.payne-gallway.co.uk/basichtml/help** for help with the hexadecimal system, or anything else about HTML!

 Set the BGCOLOR of your document to #FFFFFF or WHITE and the TEXT colour to #3366CC.

<BODY BGCOLOR=**#FFFFFF** TEXT=**#3366CC**>

What colour will the text be?

Some green

#3366CC

A tiny bit of red

Quite a lot of blue

Figure 4.9: Look at the amount of each colour being mixed

 Save your work and then see if the text looks the way that you expected!

Connecting pages

The main function of the splash page is to give people a quick, easy way to enter your web site. This is done by adding a **hyperlink** somewhere in **splash.html.**

When someone clicks on the hyperlink, the browser will go to the next page in your site.

 If you already have a Notepad window and a browser window open, **Minimise** them.

 Load up another Notepad from the **Start** Menu **(Start, Programs, Accessories, Notepad)**. Type the following in the blank new window that appears:

```
<HTML>
  <HEAD>
    <TITLE>Fee's Website:
Homepage</TITLE>
  </HEAD>
  <BODY>
    <P ALIGN=CENTER>
       This is Fee's Homepage!
    </P>
  </BODY>
</HTML>
```

Figure 4.10: A new web page

From the **File** menu choose **Save**.

In the **Save As...** window that appears, find the **My Website** folder.

Type **homepage.html** in the **File name:** box.

This step is always **VERY** important!

Set the **Save as type:** option to **All Files (*.*)**

Press the **Save** button.

Close the (new) Notepad window.

You will use this simple web page to test your first hyperlink. In Chapter 6, you will turn it into a much better page.

The <A> tag

The next step is to actually add the hyperlink.

▶ **Restore** the Notepad window that is showing your **splash.html** file.

▶ Find this paragraph:

```
<P ALIGN=CENTER>
   <IMG SRC="images/my-picture-1.jpg" WIDTH=128
HEIGHT=152>
</P>
```

▶ Add a <BR> tag after the picture of Fee, then put this text on the next line:

```
<P ALIGN=CENTER>
   <IMG SRC="images/my-picture-1.jpg" WIDTH=128
HEIGHT=152><BR>
   Click Here to Go Inside...
</P>
```

▶ Change the font of your new text to **Arial**:

```
<P ALIGN=CENTER>
   <IMG SRC="images/my-picture-1.jpg" WIDTH=128
HEIGHT=152><BR>
   <FONT FACE="arial">
     Click Here to Go Inside...
   </FONT>
</P>
```

▶ Save and take a quick look at the changes in your browser window. Then go back to Notepad.

▶ Add these <A> tags around the picture and your new text:

```
<P ALIGN=CENTER>
   <A HREF="homepage.html">
     <IMG SRC="images/my-picture-1.jpg"
WIDTH=128 HEIGHT=152><BR>
     <FONT FACE="arial">
       Click Here to Go Inside...
     </FONT>
   </A>
```

Now the picture and text are inside a new <A> section.

Test your hyperlink

 Save your work and see how the new section has affected your page. It should look just like this in your browser:

Figure 4.11: Your first link

 Click on the picture or the new text. The browser takes you to the **homepage.html** web page that you made from Figure 4.10.

 Press the **Back** button to return to **splash.html.**

The picture of Fee in Figure 4.11 suddenly has a blue border. It is easy to remove it:

 That's a number **zero,** not the letter **o.**

 Add a BORDER parameter of value 0 to the <IMG> tag in **splash.html** like this:

```
<IMG SRC="images/my-picture-1.jpg" WIDTH=128 HEIGHT=152 BORDER=0><BR>
```

 Save and refresh your page. The border has vanished, but the link still works.

How does it do that?

Hyperlinks work by using **anchors**, or <A> for short.

When you click on a hyperlink you are transported to an anchor. Anchors can be another web page or a particular point in a web page.

In **splash.html** you made a hyperlink that goes to the **homepage.html** file:

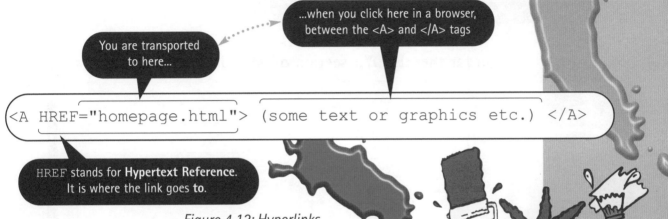

Figure 4.12: Hyperlinks

Link colours

The colour of the text inside hyperlink sections isn't affected by <FONT> tags. So how can you stop links from being bright blue all the time?

▶ Modify the <BODY> tag so it reads like this:

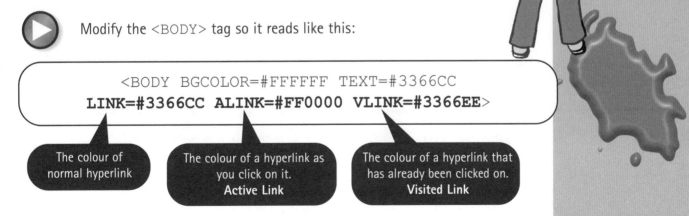

Figure 4.13: Link colours

You can try out some different colours for the Active Link (ALINK) parameter if you like.

▶ Save your work.

Chapter 5
Page Layout with Tables

So far the <BODY> section of your document is in this form:

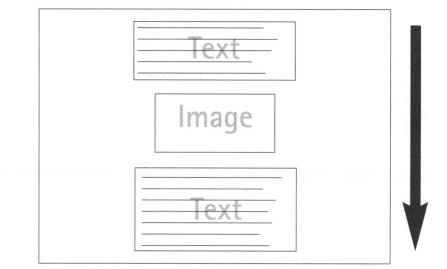

Figure 5.1: Basic layout

The page flows simply from top to bottom. It looks quite nice, but it's a bit boring!

This page below has much more interest:

Figure 5.2: A more modern layout

The best way to split a page into different sections is to use **tables**.
You will make a couple of simple tables to finish the splash page
(just to learn how they work), and then you will use your amazing
knowledge to create a **home page** in the same style as Figure 5.2.

Creating tables

 Make sure you can see the Notepad window showing **splash.html** on
the screen. Carefully follow these instructions to put everything you
have done so far into a table.

 Find the <BODY> tag. Add these three lines just after it, separated
by blank lines (to make it easy to read):

```
...
<BODY BGCOLOR=#FFFFFF TEXT=#3366CC LINK=...

    <TABLE BORDER=1 ALIGN=CENTER WIDTH=500>
      <TR>
        <TD>

<P ALIGN=CENTER>
    <FONT SIZE=5 FACE="comic sans...
```

The dots just
represent the rest
of your code -
don't actually
type them in!

Figure 5.3: Starting the table at the top of the page

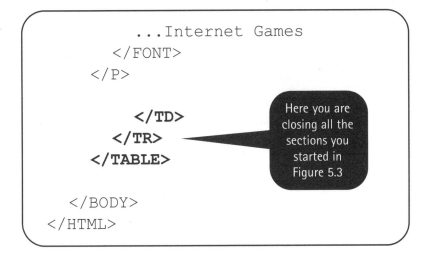 Now add these three lines just before the </BODY> tag:

```
        ...Internet Games
      </FONT>
    </P>

      </TD>
      </TR>
    </TABLE>

    </BODY>
</HTML>
```

Here you are
closing all the
sections you
started in
Figure 5.3

Figure 5.4: Closing the table at the bottom of the page

Save your file and take a peak in your browser window. It should look just like this:

Figure 5.5: One large table

Understanding the <TABLE> tags

You started the table section at the top of the body with a <TABLE> tag, and closed it right down at the bottom with the </TABLE> tag. Everything in between those two tags is inside the table, as you can see in the screenshot above.

 Look at the <TABLE> tag you added in Figure 5.3. Below it is <TR>, which stands for table row. It is closed with the </TR> tag.

 Every time you add a <TR> section, the table will gain an extra row. In the table you just made, there is only one <TR> section, so there is only one row.

Inside the <TR> section is a <TD> tag. It stands for table data, and it places one cell in your table row.

There is only one cell within the table in your **splash.html** file. The paragraphs, images and text that you typed in previous chapters are all in that one cell.

Here are some helpful diagrams to help explain how <TD>, <TR> and <TABLE> tags all fit together:

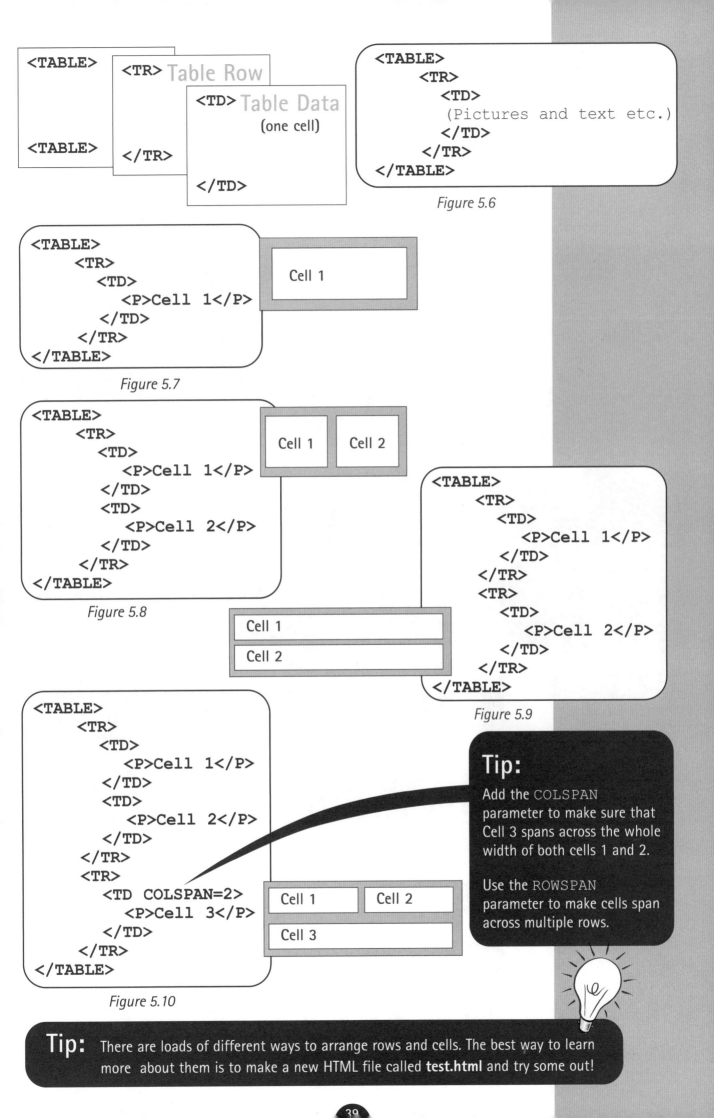

```
<TABLE>

<TABLE>
```

```
<TR> Table Row

</TR>
```

```
<TD> Table Data
(one cell)

</TD>
```

```
<TABLE>
    <TR>
      <TD>
      (Pictures and text etc.)
      </TD>
    </TR>
</TABLE>
```

Figure 5.6

```
<TABLE>
    <TR>
      <TD>
         <P>Cell 1</P>
      </TD>
    </TR>
</TABLE>
```

Cell 1

Figure 5.7

```
<TABLE>
    <TR>
      <TD>
         <P>Cell 1</P>
      </TD>
      <TD>
         <P>Cell 2</P>
      </TD>
    </TR>
</TABLE>
```

Cell 1   Cell 2

Figure 5.8

```
<TABLE>
    <TR>
      <TD>
         <P>Cell 1</P>
      </TD>
    </TR>
    <TR>
      <TD>
         <P>Cell 2</P>
      </TD>
    </TR>
</TABLE>
```

Cell 1

Cell 2

Figure 5.9

```
<TABLE>
    <TR>
      <TD>
         <P>Cell 1</P>
      </TD>
      <TD>
         <P>Cell 2</P>
      </TD>
    </TR>
    <TR>
      <TD COLSPAN=2>
         <P>Cell 3</P>
      </TD>
    </TR>
</TABLE>
```

Cell 1   Cell 2

Cell 3

Figure 5.10

Tip:

Add the COLSPAN parameter to make sure that Cell 3 spans across the whole width of both cells 1 and 2.

Use the ROWSPAN parameter to make cells span across multiple rows.

Tip: There are loads of different ways to arrange rows and cells. The best way to learn more about them is to make a new HTML file called **test.html** and try some out!

Table backgrounds

 Go back to your **splash.html** file in Notepad and change the parameters in the `<TABLE>` tag:

```
<TABLE BORDER=0 BACKGROUND="images/blue-bg.jpg" WIDTH=500>
```

Set the border width to zero

This is the other background texture that you downloaded in Chapter 2

 When you refresh your browser (after saving the file in Notepad) you should see this:

Figure 5.11: Nearly finished!

Tables within tables

The BORDER parameter of the `<TABLE>` tag doesn't really look very good, as you saw in Figure 5.5, so let's try an alternative approach!

 Add another `<TABLE>` tag outside the old one – but still within the `<BODY>` section – like this:

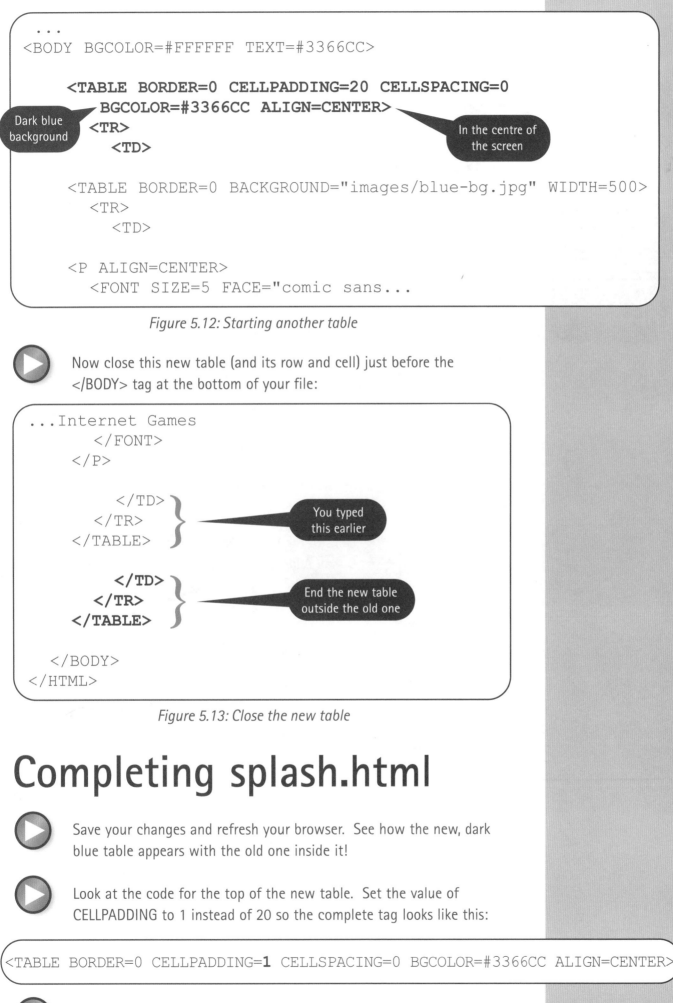

```
...
<BODY BGCOLOR=#FFFFFF TEXT=#3366CC>

    <TABLE BORDER=0 CELLPADDING=20 CELLSPACING=0
     BGCOLOR=#3366CC ALIGN=CENTER>
    <TR>
      <TD>

    <TABLE BORDER=0 BACKGROUND="images/blue-bg.jpg" WIDTH=500>
      <TR>
        <TD>

    <P ALIGN=CENTER>
      <FONT SIZE=5 FACE="comic sans...
```

Dark blue background

In the centre of the screen

Figure 5.12: Starting another table

▶ Now close this new table (and its row and cell) just before the
</BODY> tag at the bottom of your file:

```
...Internet Games
      </FONT>
    </P>

        </TD>
      </TR>
    </TABLE>

      </TD>
    </TR>
  </TABLE>

  </BODY>
</HTML>
```

You typed this earlier

End the new table outside the old one

Figure 5.13: Close the new table

Completing splash.html

▶ Save your changes and refresh your browser. See how the new, dark blue table appears with the old one inside it!

▶ Look at the code for the top of the new table. Set the value of CELLPADDING to 1 instead of 20 so the complete tag looks like this:

```
<TABLE BORDER=0 CELLPADDING=1 CELLSPACING=0 BGCOLOR=#3366CC ALIGN=CENTER>
```

▶ The page now looks like Figure 2.1.

If you can't quite get your head around the last bit about the tables, go to **www.payne-gallway.co.uk/basichtml/code** and click on the **splash.html** link. It shows the code for the whole page so that you can see where you went wrong.

Site plan

Now that you know the basics of HTML and have completed your splash page, it is important to plan the rest of your site.

This flow diagram shows the structure you will use:

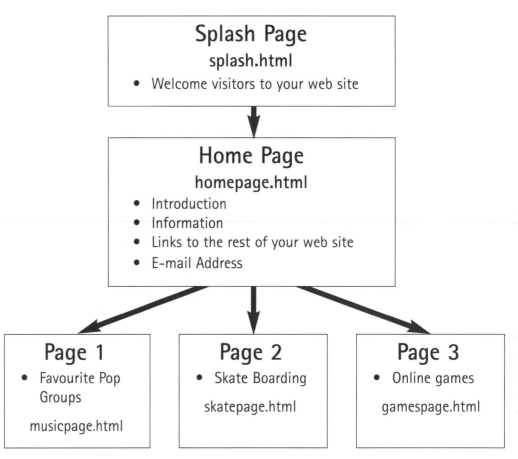

Figure 5.14: Site Plan

Once everything is finished you can change these pages to anything you like, but stick to the examples in here for now.

Chapter 6
Building your Home Page

 Close any windows that you don't really need.

Load up a new **Notepad** from the **Start** menu and open the file called **homepage.html** from the **My Website** folder.

Make sure that it looks just like this:

Note:

When you open an HTML file using Notepad, don't forget to select **All Files (*.*)** from the list called **Files of type**.

```
homepage.html - Notepad                    _ □ ×
File   Edit   Search   Help
<HTML>
  <HEAD>
    <TITLE>Fee's Website: Homepage</TITLE>
  </HEAD>
  <BODY>
    <P ALIGN=CENTER>
      This is Fee's Homepage!
    </P>
  </BODY>
</HTML>
```

Figure 6.1: The homepage.html file

Now you are going to make some **big** changes. This page will be the centre of your web site, so it has to be good!

 Take a quick glance a Figure 5.2. **Homepage.html** will use a similar style.

 Delete the only paragraph section using Notepad.

Now add a table so the entire file looks like this:

```
<HTML>
  <HEAD>
    <TITLE>Fee's Website: Homepage</TITLE>
  </HEAD>
  <BODY>
    <TABLE WIDTH=750 ALIGN=CENTER BORDER=0 CELLPADDING=0 CELLSPACING=0>
      <TR>
        <TD WIDTH=250 VALIGN=TOP BGCOLOR=#AAAAFF>
          menu
        </TD>
        <TD VALIGN=TOP BGCOLOR=#DDDDFF>
          main section
        </TD>
      </TR>
    </TABLE>
  </BODY>
```

The whole table is 750 pixels wide

Figure 6.2: Make sure you haven't made any mistakes

Check **homepage.html** page in your browser now:

The whole table is 750 pixels wide

Figure 6.3: Can you see why it looks like this?

You should see a table that has one row (because you only made one `<TR>` section). This row is split into two cells. The first cell is 250 pixels wide, and the second cell fills the rest of the space.

Comments

It is a good idea to label each different part of the code with **comment** tags. Anything between the `<!--` and `-->` tags will be ignored by the browser:

```
<!-- this is a little comment -->
```

Add two comments to **homepage.html**:

```
        <TD WIDTH=250 VALIGN=TOP BGCOLOR=#AAAAFF>
<!-- menu section -->
        menu
... (more code)
<!-- main section -->
        main section
```

Figure 6.4: Add comments at the top of the menu section and the main section

 Save the file and refresh your browser.

You won't see any changes! Comments are **invisible** tags - they're just there to help you find your way around your HTML code.

Preparing the graphics

 Connect to the Internet and open the page
www.payne-gallway.co.uk/basichtml/graphics

 Click on the link called **Images for homepage.html** and wait for the page to load completely.

Download **every single image**, even the little animations, following this procedure:

 Right-click on a picture and select **Save Picture As...**

In the dialog box that appears, find your **Images** folder inside **My Website**. Press **Save** and then repeat the process for all the other pictures on the page.

Double-click on the **My Computer** icon on your **Desktop** and find your **Images** folder.

You should have all these files inside it:

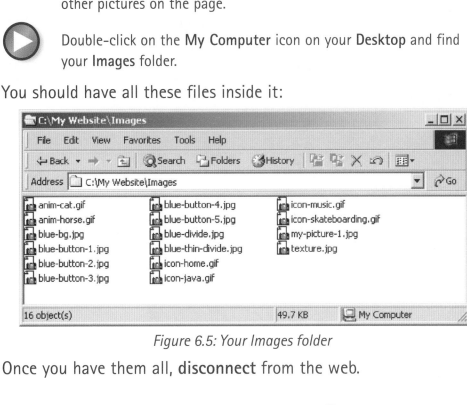

Figure 6.5: Your Images folder

Once you have them all, **disconnect** from the web.

Note:
This might take you about ten minutes or so.

The icons might look a bit different on your screen.

A title for the Menu cell

 Find where you typed `<!-- menu section -->`

▶ Delete the word `menu` (just below the comment) and replace it with a new table:

```
    ...
        <TD WIDTH=250 VALIGN=TOP BGCOLOR=#AAAAFF>
<!-- menu section -->
        <TABLE WIDTH=150 BORDER=0 BGCOLOR=#3366CC CELLSPACING=0
            CELLMARGIN=1 ALIGN=CENTER>
        <TR>
          <TD ALIGN=RIGHT HEIGHT=22>
            <FONT COLOR=WHITE FACE="arial" SIZE=4>Welcome to</FONT>
          </TD>
        </TR>
        </TABLE>
        </TD>
    ...
```

*Figure 6.6: Replace **menu** with a little table*

▶ Select **Save** from the **File** menu, and then **Refresh** the page in your browser.

You should see a new table nested inside the original one:

| Welcome to | main section |

Figure 6.7: Nested tables

Make sure you understand why the table looks like this!

Go back to Notepad. You need to do two things now.

 Change the background colour of the first cell of the big table to WHITE.

 Then add a paragraph just below the little table (but still inside the main table) like this:

```
...
   <TD WIDTH=250 VALIGN=TOP BGCOLOR=WHITE>
<!-- menu section -->
      <TABLE WIDTH=150 BORDER=0 BGCOLOR=#3366CC CELLSPACING=0
           CELLMARGIN=1 ALIGN=CENTER>
       <TR>
         <TD ALIGN=RIGHT HEIGHT=22>
            <FONT COLOR=WHITE FACE="arial" SIZE=4>Welcome to</FONT>
         </TD>
       </TR>
      </TABLE>

      <P ALIGN=CENTER>
        <FONT FACE="comic sans ms,arial" SIZE=5><B>Fee's Website!
            </B></FONT>
         <BR>
         <IMG SRC="images/blue-divide.jpg">
      </P>
   </TD>
...
```

Figure 6.8: All of the above code is just for the left cell of the main table

 Select **Save** from the **File** menu, and then **Refresh** the page in your browser.

The paragraph should appear just below the new table, and the background for that whole side of the main table should be white.

Welcome to | main section

Fee's Website!

Figure 6.9: The page is taking shape

Making a menu

 Return to your Notepad window showing **homepage.html**.

 Type this comment just after the paragraph you added.

```
...
            <IMG SRC="images/blue-divide.jpg">
        </P>
<!-- menu -->
        </TD>
    ...
```

You are about to add a menu. It will contain five links to other parts of your web site. Type these two paragraphs just after the `<!-- menu -->` comment:

```
<!-- menu -->
    <P ALIGN=LEFT>
      <FONT FACE="arial">
        <A HREF="homepage.html">Homepage</A><BR>
        <A HREF="musicpage.html">Music</A><BR>
        <A HREF="skatepage.html">Skate Boarding</A><BR>
        <A HREF="gamespage.html">JAVA Games</A><BR>
        <A HREF="mailto:fee@webtribe.net">E-Mail</A><BR>
      </FONT>
    </P>

    <P ALIGN=CENTER>
      <IMG SRC="images/blue-divide.jpg">
    </P>
    </TD>
```

Figure 6.10: Code for the menu

Check out your home page now.

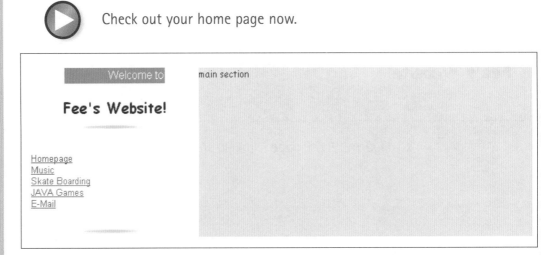

Figure 6.11: Note how the <A> and <BR> tags have arranged the links

Smart graphics

In Notepad, find the links you just made. They are all together in one paragraph.

Add these <IMG> tags inside each link:

```
<A HREF="homepage.html">
<IMG SRC="images/blue-button-1.jpg" ALIGN=MIDDLE BORDER=0>
Homepage</A><BR>
<A HREF="musicpage.html">
<IMG SRC="images/blue-button-2.jpg" ALIGN=MIDDLE BORDER=0>
Music</A><BR>
<A HREF="skatepage.html">
<IMG SRC="images/blue-button-3.jpg" ALIGN=MIDDLE BORDER=0>
Skate Boarding</A><BR>
<A HREF="gamespage.html">
<IMG SRC="images/blue-button-4.jpg" ALIGN=MIDDLE BORDER=0>
JAVA Games</A><BR>
<A HREF="mailto:feeonline@webtribe.net">
<IMG SRC="images/blue-button-5.jpg" ALIGN=MIDDLE BORDER=0>
E-Mail</A><BR>
```

Now see how the menu has been transformed, simply by adding some graphics:

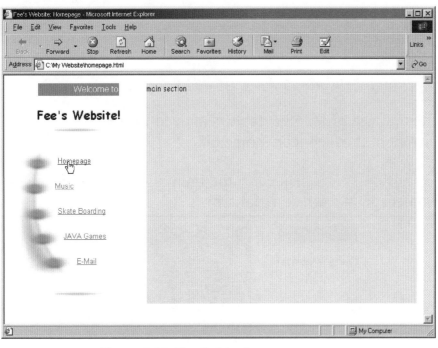

Figure 6.12: The finished menu

So how are we going to set about the main section of the home page?

More tables

 Find the `<!-- main section -->` comment in **homepage.html**:

```
...
        <TD VALIGN=TOP BGCOLOR=#DDDDFF>
<!-- main section -->
            main section
        </TD>
    ...
```

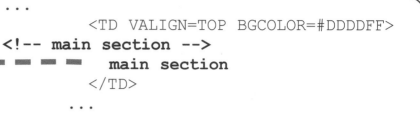 Set the `BGCOLOR` parameter of the cell to `#3366CC`, and replace the text `main section` with a new table:

```
...
    <TD VALIGN=TOP BGCOLOR=#3366CC>
<!-- main section -->
        <TABLE BGCOLOR=#3366CC CELLSPACING=1 BORDER=0 WIDTH=500>
          <TR HEIGHT=28>
            <TD ALIGN=LEFT>
              <IMG SRC="images/icon-home.gif">
            </TD>
            <TD ALIGN=RIGHT>
              <FONT COLOR=WHITE FACE="arial" SIZE=4>Homepage</FONT>
            </TD>
          </TR>
        </TABLE>
    </TD>
    ...
```

Figure 6.13: A new table with one row and two cells

The first cell of the new table is aligned to the left. It has a little picture in it called **icon-home.gif**.

The second cell is aligned to the right, and it contains the word **Homepage** in a **white, Arial** font:

Figure 6.14: Starting to look better...

To start making use of the great big blue area, simply add another
row to the new table:

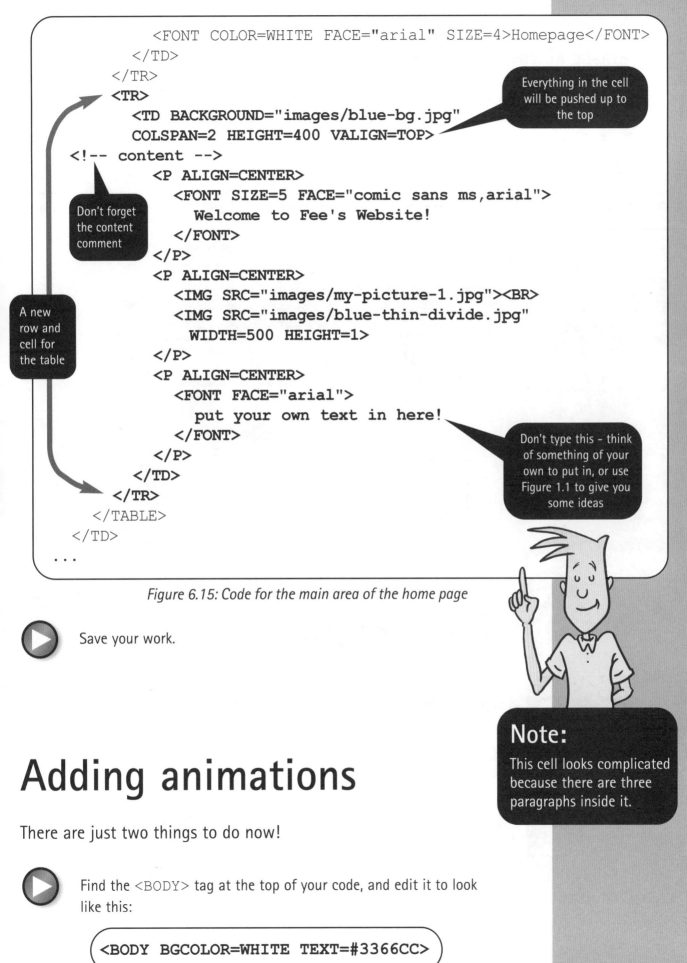

```
            <FONT COLOR=WHITE FACE="arial" SIZE=4>Homepage</FONT>
        </TD>
    </TR>
    <TR>
        <TD BACKGROUND="images/blue-bg.jpg"
        COLSPAN=2 HEIGHT=400 VALIGN=TOP>
<!-- content -->
        <P ALIGN=CENTER>
            <FONT SIZE=5 FACE="comic sans ms,arial">
            Welcome to Fee's Website!
            </FONT>
        </P>
        <P ALIGN=CENTER>
            <IMG SRC="images/my-picture-1.jpg"><BR>
            <IMG SRC="images/blue-thin-divide.jpg"
            WIDTH=500 HEIGHT=1>
        </P>
        <P ALIGN=CENTER>
            <FONT FACE="arial">
            put your own text in here!
            </FONT>
        </P>
        </TD>
    </TR>
    </TABLE>
    </TD>
...
```

Everything in the cell
will be pushed up to
the top

Don't forget
the content
comment

A new
row and
cell for
the table

Don't type this - think
of something of your
own to put in, or use
Figure 1.1 to give you
some ideas

Figure 6.15: Code for the main area of the home page

Save your work.

Note:
This cell looks complicated
because there are three
paragraphs inside it.

Adding animations

There are just two things to do now!

Find the <BODY> tag at the top of your code, and edit it to look
like this:

```
<BODY BGCOLOR=WHITE TEXT=#3366CC>
```

51

Now type the new code from Figure 6.16 just below the body tag - right at the top of the web page (it's the last table, I promise!)

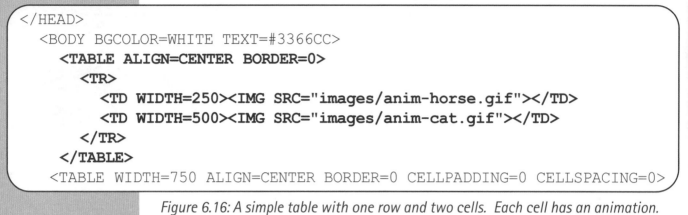

```
</HEAD>
  <BODY BGCOLOR=WHITE TEXT=#3366CC>
    <TABLE ALIGN=CENTER BORDER=0>
      <TR>
        <TD WIDTH=250><IMG SRC="images/anim-horse.gif"></TD>
        <TD WIDTH=500><IMG SRC="images/anim-cat.gif"></TD>
      </TR>
    </TABLE>
    <TABLE WIDTH=750 ALIGN=CENTER BORDER=0 CELLPADDING=0 CELLSPACING=0>
```

Figure 6.16: A simple table with one row and two cells. Each cell has an animation.

Save **homepage.html** again and take a look in your browser – you've made a great page!

Figure 6.17: Fee's home page

New graphics

If you don't like those animations, there are plenty of others at
www.payne-gallway.co.uk/basichtml/animations
so download a couple to your **Images** folder in the usual way.

It is easy to use a scanned photo of yourself, or a picture from the web, on your pages instead of the pictures of Fee.

Make sure they are saved in the JPEG graphics format (.jpg), then put them in your **Images** folder.

Find out the width and height of the pictures (in pixels) and then modify the relevant <IMG> tags.

Make sure you check out
www.payne-gallway.co.uk/basichtml/graphics/new for some great ideas about how to improve the look of your site.

Tip:
To change graphics format, open the picture in Microsoft Paint or any other image-editing program and use **Export** or **Save As** to convert the file to a (.jpg) JPEG image.

Chapter 7
Multimedia

How do you fancy adding some videos, sounds and maybe even a game to your site?

Copying homepage.html

 Open up **homepage.html** from **My Website** if it's not already on your screen.

 Select **Save As...** from the **File** menu. This will make a copy of **homepage.html** with a different name. In the dialogue box that has appeared, do the following:

 Make sure the **Save in:** box is showing the **My Website** folder.

Change **Save as type:** to **All Files (*.*)**.

Type **musicpage.html** into the **File name:** box and then press **Save** to create the new file.

The Notepad window title should now look like this:

```
musicpage.html - Notepad                    _ □ X
```

Figure 7.1: The current file is now musicpage.html

Wave sound

There are four main audio formats that you can use in your webpages:

Format	Good Points	Bad Points
MP3	High quality and low file size - excellent for music	You need to download special software to create MP3 files
WAV	Easy to make and high quality - good for short bursts of music	Large file size (so they take a while to download)
MIDI	Very tiny file size	MIDIs don't store real sounds - they just play complex sequences of notes
µLAW	Tiny file size - good for simple sounds	Very poor sound quality

You'll use a WAV file for a simple background sound.

 Go to **www.payne-gallway.co.uk/basichtml/sounds** in your browser and download **drums.wav** by right-clicking on the link and saving the file to the **Sounds** folder in **My Website**.

 In Notepad (which is now showing **musicpage.html**) find the <BODY> tag and type:

```
. . .
</HEAD>
 <BODY BGCOLOR=WHITE  TEXT=#3366CC>
   <EMBED SRC="sounds/drums.wav" AUTOSTART=TRUE
   LOOP=FALSE ALIGN=CENTER WIDTH=1  HEIGHT=1>
   </EMBED>
  <TABLE ALIGN=CENTER BORDER=0>
    <TR>
     <TD WIDTH=250><IMG SRC="images/anim-horse.gif"></TD>
. . .
```

Figure 7.2: The <EMBED> tag for sounds

Tip:

For some reason, the sound won't play if the width or height is less than 1, so leave them like this.

You can make sounds play over and over again by setting the LOOP parameter to TRUE.

AUTOSTART must always be TRUE. You never really need to change the alignment, the width or the height because sounds are invisible.

 Open **homepage.html** in your browser and click the **Music** link on the menu. You'll hear drums.

Tip:

If you don't hear any sound check that your speakers are on!

The music page looks exactly the same as the home page, though, doesn't it?

Go through the code changing all the titles and things to **Music**.

 Write about your favourite band and add some pictures just after the `<!-- content -->` comment in your code.

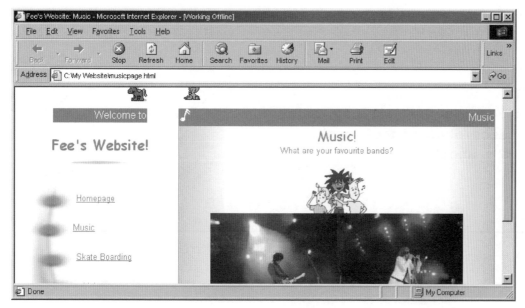

Figure 7.3: Fee's Music Page looks like this

To learn more about using sounds in HTML, read the rest of the information on **www.payne-gallway.co.uk/basichtml/sounds** and try the examples!

Video clips

 Select **Open...** from the **File** menu and load **homepage.html**.

 Follow the **Copying homepage.html** procedure from the first page of this chapter, but this time create a file called **skatepage.html** instead of **musicpage.html**.

Note:
If you're not really into skateboarding, you can rename **skatepage.html** to something different later on. Don't forget to change all of the links on the home page and everywhere else so that they point to the new file name!

Find the `<!-- content -->` comment and add this code after it:

```
<!-- content -->
  <P ALIGN=CENTER>
    <EMBED SRC="videos/skatevideo1.mpg" AUTOSTART=TRUE WIDTH=320
                                        HEIGHT=192 LOOP=FALSE>

    </EMBED>
  </P>
  <P ALIGN=CENTER>
    <A HREF="http://www.payne-gallway.co.uk
    /basichtml/videos/skatevideo2.mpg">
      Click here for another video!
    </A>
  </P>
  ...
```

Figure 7.4: Code for video clips

Figure 7.5: Fee's Video Page

The `<EMBED>` tag has been used again – but this time for a video instead of sound.

Go to **www.payne-gallway.co.uk/basichtml/videos** for more information.

Java

You can add some Java games to your website:

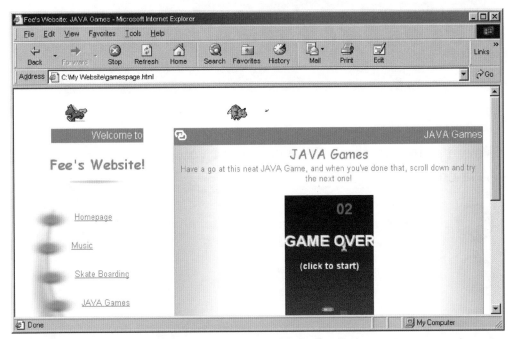

Figure 7.6

The object you must add to insert a game is called a **Java Applet**.
Here is a simple example:

 Go to **www.payne-gallway.co.uk/basichtml/java** and download the
file **game1.class** by right-clicking on its name and saving it to
My Website.

 Go through the **Copying homepage.html** procedure again and create
a file called **gamespage.html**.

Add this paragraph just after the `<!-- content -->` comment:

```
<!-- content -->
    <P ALIGN=CENTER>
      <APPLET CODE="game1.class" WIDTH=300 HEIGHT=250>
      </APPLET>
    </P>
    ...
```

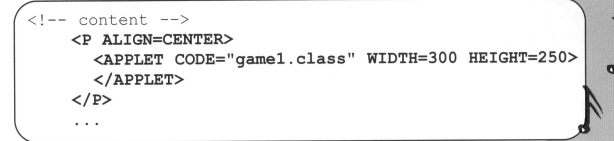

Figure 7.7: Add a Java Applet

To find some better games, see
www.payne-gallway.co.uk/basichtml/java and try the
other examples.

 Customise the rest of **gamespage.html** to your satisfaction.

Tip:
Some are easy to
add to a web
page, others are
quite tricky!

Chapter 8
Uploading by FTP

Now it's time to show the world what you have created!

 Open up your browser and connect to the internet.

 Go to **www.portland.co.uk**

Getting space on the web

Note:

You don't *have* to use **Portland.co.uk** for your web site! Any **ISP** (Internet Service Provider) which lets you use **FTP** will also work just fine!

For example you could use one of these:

www.lycos.com
www.tripod.com
www.freeserve.co.uk

Figure 8.1: A free web host

 Click on the **Free Web Hosting** link, or the **Hosting** option from the menu on the right.

A new page should appear as shown in Figure 8.2. Click on the **FREE Webhosting** link and wait for that page to load.

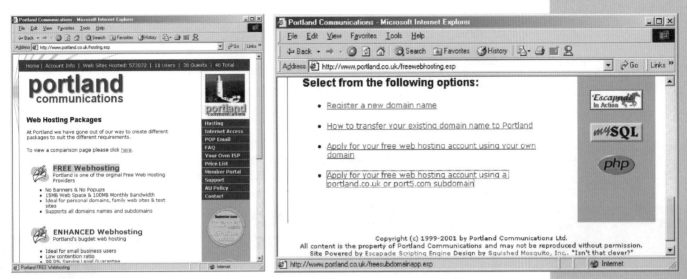

Figure 8.2

Figure 8.3

 Scroll down to the bottom of the new page. Click on the link which allows you to use a **subdomain**, shown at the bottom of Figure 8.3.

 A web page like Figure 8.4 will appear. Type a name for your web site, and choose an ending from the list.

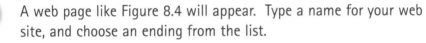 Type your e-mail address in the second text area.

Note:
Using a subdomain means that your web site will be stored on the Portland webserver as part of their internet 'domain'.

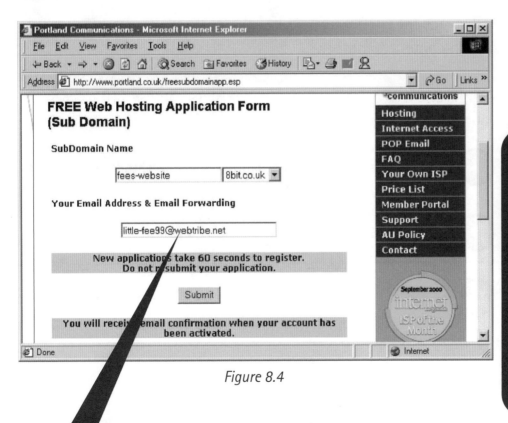

Figure 8.4

Tip:
Keep the SubDomain name quite short and do not use spaces or any punctuation. You *can* use a hyphen "-" or an underscore "_" if you like. If you are doing this in class, type the name of your school, your year and your first name. For example **woodbridge-year9-kate**

If you do not have an e-mail address, you can either type in a friend's address and ask them to tell you the details that are sent there, or go to **www.payne-gallway.co.uk/basichtml/getemail** to find out how to get an e-mail address of your own.

59

As you can see, Fee's web site address will be **fees-website.8bit.co.uk**

 When you're ready, press the **Submit** button and a username and password will shortly be sent to you by e-mail. You will need them to upload your web pages.

Main Page | Hosting | Account Info | Member Portal | Sites Hosted

portland
communications

Adding subdomain 'fees-website.8bit.co.uk' for Portland Communications Ltd

Successfully created subdomain 'fees-website.8bit.co.uk'.

You will receive a confirmation email containing your user ID and password shortly.

The new name for your web site, your **web address**, will appear here. Write this down, too!

Figure 8.5: Now you've got a place on the internet to save your web site!

Loading an FTP Client

FTP stands for File Transfer Protocol. It's a way to copy files from one computer to another.

An FTP Client is a special program that lets you use FTP to copy your web site from your computer onto the internet.

 Open the page **www.payne-gallway.co.uk/basichtml/programs** and click on the link called **FileZilla**.

Use the instructions there to download and install the FileZilla FTP Client.

 Once it's installed, double-click on the FileZilla icon on your desktop.

FileZilla

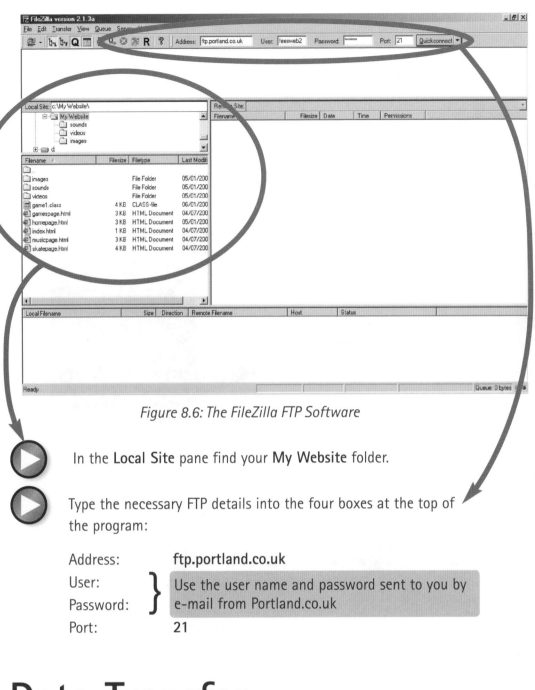

Figure 8.6: The FileZilla FTP Software

 In the **Local Site** pane find your **My Website** folder.

 Type the necessary FTP details into the four boxes at the top of the program:

Address:	**ftp.portland.co.uk**
User:	Use the user name and password sent to you by
Password:	e-mail from Portland.co.uk
Port:	**21**

Data Transfer

Connect to the internet.

Check that the FTP details are correct, then click **Quickconnect**. ——

Some information will appear in the uppermost white space in the FileZilla program window. It continually gives details on how it is communicating with the Portland.co.uk server.

Eventually a couple of icons should appear in the **Remote Site** pane.

Tip:
Maximise the program window so that everything is easier to see.

Quickconnect ▼

Tip:
If nothing has happened after five minutes, check that you entered the correct FTP details and try again.

All you need to do to upload your web site is drag each file in the **Local Site** pane to the **Remote Site** pane. It's as easy as that!

 Start by dragging **gamespage.html** across into the **Remote Pane**.

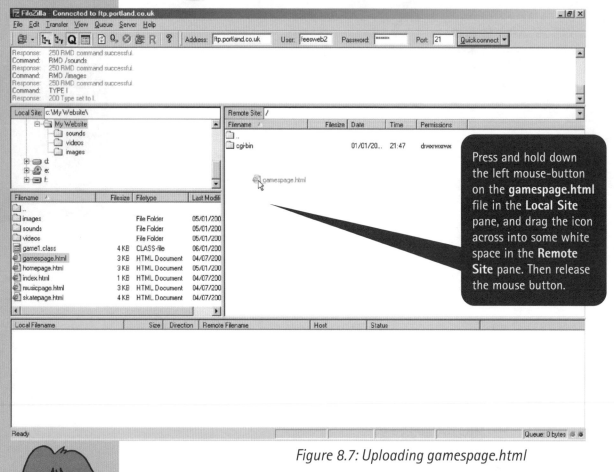

> Press and hold down the left mouse-button on the **gamespage.html** file in the **Local Site** pane, and drag the icon across into some white space in the **Remote Site** pane. Then release the mouse button.

Figure 8.7: Uploading gamespage.html

Do the same thing for all the other HTML files and the Java game.

Then drag the **Images**, **Sounds** and **Videos** folders across to the **Remote Site** pane one by one.

Tip:

Your folders have files inside them, so they will take longer to upload. A progress bar will appear in the bottom pane to show you how much has been completed.

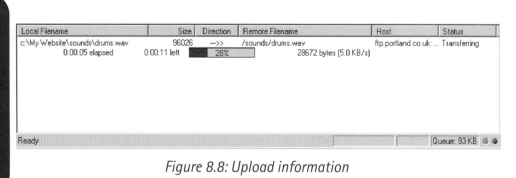

Figure 8.8: Upload information

F5 ———— Once you have uploaded all files and folders, press the **F5** key at the top of your keyboard to refresh the **Remote Site** pane.

Double-click the **Images** folder in the **Remote** pane and check that everything is there. ——— images

 Check that all the files have the same sizes as in the **Local** pane. Double click on the **..** icon to leave the **Images** folder. ——— ..

 Do the same checks in the **Sounds** and **Videos** remote folders as well.

Tip:
If some of them don't have the correct file sizes, simply drag them across again!

Disconnect

When you are confident that everything has been copied across properly you can disconnect from the Internet.

 Select **Disconnect** from the **File** menu to close the **FTP** connection. Then exit the FileZilla program.

Fee's web address is **fees-website.8bit.co.uk** (see Figure 8.5).

 View your web site by typing *your* new web address into the address bar of a browser window.

Figure 8.9: Check out your finished web site on the internet!

 Is everything there? If not, reopen the FTP client and upload any missing pages or pictures.

 Disconnect from the internet.

Congratulations! You're on the way to becoming an HTML expert.

Index

\<A\>	33
\<BODY\>	11
\<BR\>	15
\<EMBED\>	54
\<FONT\>	22, 24, 27
\<HEAD\>	10
\<HTML\>	10
\<IMG\>	18, 49
\<P\>	11
\<TABLE\>	38
\<TD\>	37, 38
\<TITLE\>	10
\<TR\>	37, 38
µLAW	54
ALIGN parameter	13
ALINK	35
anchors	35
animation	51
applet	57
audio formats	54
background	20
background colour	25
BGCOLOR	25, 26
bold text	21
BORDER	34
browser	4, 7
comment tags	44
data transfer	61
download images	45
FireWorks	5
Flash	6
folder	
creating	8
Images	8
renaming	8
Sounds	8
Videos	8
font	
face	23
size	23
FrontPage	5
FTP client	60
games	57
google.com	3
graphics	16
hexadecimal	
colours	29
numbers	28
HREF	35
HTML	2
hyperlink	32
image size	19
Internet Explorer	4, 7
italic text	21
Java	57
JPEG graphics format	52
line break	15
link	35, 48
link colours	35
menu	48
MIDI	54
MP3	54
multimedia	53
music page	54
new line	15
Notepad	4, 7
parameters	13
Portland.co.uk	58
preset colours	25
Publisher	5
refreshing the page	14
search engine	3
server	3
site plan	42
sounds	54
splash page	9
tag	
end	10
start	10
tags	9
text colour	27
text editor	4, 7
textured background	20
underlined text	21
upload	62
video clips	55
viewing in a browser	12
VLINK	35
WAV	54
wave sounds	54
web page	3
web site	3
Word	5
WordPerfect	5